Ahoy there, kids! Ready to sing the
SpongeBob SquarePants theme song?
I can't hear you!
OOOOOOOOOOOOOOOOH,
Who lives in a pineapple under the sea?
SpongeBob SquarePants!
Absorbent and yellow and porous is he.
SpongeBob SquarePants!
If nautical nonsense be something you wish.
SpongeBob SquarePants!
Then drop on the deck and flop like a fish.
SpongeBob SquarePants!
SpongeBob SquarePants!
SpongeBob SquarePants!
SpongeBob SquarePants!
Sponge— Bob,   Square— Pants!
Ah ha ha ha ah har har har

Hall Monitor

Mrs. Puff sighed deeply. "All right, I guess I have no choice." She gulped. "The hall monitor of the week is . . . SpongeBob."

"Ya-HOOOO!" yelled SpongeBob.

And so the victory dance began. SpongeBob raced around the classroom, bouncing off the walls and zigzagging around the desks. All the while he shouted, "Hall monitor! Hall monitor! I'm the hall monitor!"

Finally SpongeBob calmed down, stood next to Mrs. Puff in the front of the class, and saluted. "Hall Monitor SpongeBob reporting for duty, ma'am," he said in a drill sergeant voice.

Mrs. Puff began, "Now Sp—"

But SpongeBob continued. "I'm ready to assume my position . . . IN THE HALL!"

"Yes, but—," Mrs. Puff said.

"I will protect all who are weak . . . IN THE HALL!" SpongeBob shouted. "All rules will be enforced IN THE HALL!"

"Okay!" said an annoyed Mrs. Puff. "Just take the cap and belt."

"I can't accept that yet, ma'am," SpongeBob told her. "First I have to make my speech."

Based on the TV series *SpongeBob SquarePants*®
created by Stephen Hillenburg as seen on Nickelodeon®

ISBN 0-439-19375-3

12 11 10 9 8 7 6 5 4 3 2   1 2 3 4 5 6/0

Printed in the U.S.A.

First Scholastic printing, November 2001

Hall Monitor

by **Annie Auerbach**

based on an original teleplay by
**Chuck Klein, Jay Lender,
and Mr. Lawrence**

illustrated by **Mark O'Hare**

SCHOLASTIC INC.
New York Toronto London Auckland Sydney
Mexico City New Delhi Hong Kong Buenos Aires

chapter one

There's no one in Bikini Bottom quite like SpongeBob SquarePants. When he's not at work flipping Krabby Patties or on an adventure with his best friend, Patrick, SpongeBob can be found at Mrs. Puff's Boating School. Mrs. Puff's Boating School is where students learn the rules of the road.

SpongeBob has taken Mrs. Puff's class forty-seven times. He knows the answer to *every* question *in* the classroom. But when it's time for the driving portion of the exam, SpongeBob always panics behind the wheel and ends up failing. When SpongeBob is on the road, it's best to steer clear—or run for cover!

One day at school, things seemed normal: SpongeBob sat in the back of the class taking precise notes while all the other students slept. Their snoring was almost louder than Mrs. Puff's lecture.

"Everyone wake up!" Mrs. Puff called. "It's time to pick this week's hall monitor."

SpongeBob's sat upright in his seat. He moved his desk out into the center aisle to make sure Mrs. Puff could see him. Being chosen as hall monitor was an honor SpongeBob wanted more than anything. With his eyes wide and hopeful, he wished hard for his name to be called.

Mrs. Puff looked down at the list attached to

her clipboard and said, "Let's see here . . . this week's hall monitor will be . . . um . . . Bart. No, he's done it already. Tina? No, no," she said to herself. Then Mrs. Puff gasped in horror. At the bottom of the list was the name she feared the most: SpongeBob SquarePants!

"It's Jimmy! Jimmy's the hall monitor!" Mrs. Puff exclaimed.

Jimmy, a green fish wearing shorts and a T-shirt, shook his head and said, "Mrs. Puff, I've done it already."

"Oh!" Mrs. Puff replied, quickly scanning the list again. "Bill?"

"No way, Mrs. Puff!" answered Bill, a plump gray fish sitting in the back.

Mrs. Puff wasted no time. "Tina, you're the hall monitor," she said.

"Hey! I've done it three times already," Tina declared, her fins on her hips.

"Uh . . . B-Beth!" Mrs. Puff said. "Yes, Beth!"

"She graduated," Jimmy told her.

By this time, SpongeBob had eagerly inched his desk up the aisle. He could hardly contain his excitement. He knew what was coming.

But Mrs. Puff was still trying to avoid calling the name of a certain rectangular student. "Henry? Vera? Sheldon?" she called out in desperation.

But it was no use.

Mrs. Puff sighed deeply. "All right, I guess I have no choice." She gulped. "The hall monitor of the week is . . . SpongeBob."

"Ya-HOOOO!" yelled SpongeBob.

And so the victory dance began. SpongeBob raced around the classroom, bouncing off the walls and zigzagging around the desks. All the while he shouted, "Hall monitor! Hall monitor! I'm the hall monitor!"

Finally SpongeBob calmed down, stood next to Mrs. Puff in the front of the class, and saluted. "Hall Monitor SpongeBob reporting for duty, ma'am," he said in a drill sergeant voice.

Mrs. Puff began, "Now Sp—"

But SpongeBob continued. "I'm ready to assume my position . . . IN THE HALL!"

"Yes, but—," Mrs. Puff said.

"I will protect all who are weak . . . IN THE HALL!" SpongeBob shouted. "All rules will be enforced IN THE HALL!"

"Okay!" said an annoyed Mrs. Puff. "Just take the cap and belt."

"I can't accept that yet, ma'am," SpongeBob told her. "First I have to make my speech."

Mrs. Puff sighed. "You can't make this easy, can you?"

"CLASSMATES!" SpongeBob began. "Who am I to deserve such a great honor? Why, I'd be nothing without Mrs. Puff."

"Oh, give me a break," Mrs. Puff muttered under her breath.

". . . and to my public," SpongeBob continued, "all I can say is . . . well, frankly, I'm touched." He wiped a tear away. "I want you to know that I represent *you* out there . . . out there IN THE HALL. I will carry out my duties . . . ," SpongeBob promised as he rambled on. ". . . crime and punishment . . . punishment and crime . . . IN THE HALL."

The other students sighed and groaned.

But SpongeBob wasn't done. "That reminds me of an extremely long speech written by the greatest hall monitor of all time." He took a dramatic pause. "Friends, students, juvenile delinquents . . . lend me your ears . . ."

The students covered their ears.

Three hours later, SpongeBob was getting ready to wrap up his speech. Finally he said, "In conclusion, and without a moment to spare, I will put on this uniform and assume my duties as . . . hall monitor!"

SpongeBob had expected a round of applause. But by this time everyone had fallen asleep—including Mrs. Puff. Luckily, the bell rang.

"Zzzzzz . . . huh? Oh!" Mrs. Puff said as she stood up.

All the students woke up with a jolt and rushed out of the classroom. They practically ran right over SpongeBob on their way out.

"SpongeBob, are you okay?" Mrs. Puff asked.

SpongeBob sighed. "I overdid the speech again, didn't I?" he asked his teacher.

"I'm afraid so," Mrs. Puff told him.

"Aw, tartar sauce!" exclaimed SpongeBob. "I guess I won't be needing these." He handed the hall monitor cap and belt back to his teacher. "I hardly knew ya," he added, looking sadly at the uniform.

SpongeBob was gripping the uniform so tightly that Mrs. Puff had to pry it from his hands. SpongeBob's disappointment showed in his face, as well as in his slightly deflated head.

Mrs. Puff couldn't believe it, but she actually felt sorry for SpongeBob. Each time he'd been elected hall monitor, he hadn't made it out the door. "Uh . . . SpongeBob?"

"Yes, Mrs. Puff?" replied SpongeBob.

"I can at least let you *wear* the uniform until tomorrow," she offered.

"Woo-hoo!" yelled SpongeBob. His head was instantly back to its full size. "Thanks, Mrs. Puff!"

SpongeBob sang to himself as he put on his hall monitor uniform. "Be bop de diddit de doo . . . hall be bop be diddle monitor . . . root toot toot."

Mrs. Puff sighed and shook her head as SpongeBob bounded out the classroom door.

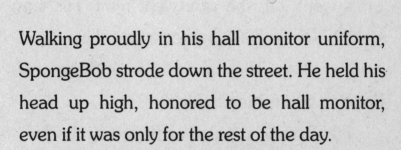

chapter two

Walking proudly in his hall monitor uniform, SpongeBob strode down the street. He held his head up high, honored to be hall monitor, even if it was only for the rest of the day.

Suddenly he stopped dead in his tracks. "A broken traffic light!" he cried. "Hmmm . . . who's to say my monitoring duties should end just because the bell rang?" he wondered. Then he straightened his cap. "I can be helpful anywhere! Yes, this looks like a job for the hall monitor!"

SpongeBob pulled out a whistle. "All right," he said as he signaled. "Hey, big boat, you go that way, and this turbo boat can go this way, and this one that way, and this one left . . . and this one right . . . and over here . . . and over there . . ."

SpongeBob not only made signals with his arms, but with his legs and rear end as well! His arms went left, the cars went right. His legs kicked out, the cars swerved around! No driver could follow. They weren't sure if he was dancing or directing traffic.

"Ha! This is a piece of Krusty Krabcake!" SpongeBob said confidently.

Just then, two boats swiped each side of SpongeBob, sending him spinning. *"Whoa!"* he yelled.

Gaining his balance, SpongeBob looked up to see a huge boat coming right toward him!

With all his might, SpongeBob stretched his legs as far as they would go, just in the nick of time.

"Yikes!" SpongeBob yelled and the big boat zoomed right between his legs.

"Barnacle brain!" yelled the driver.

SpongeBob couldn't really hear him over the traffic noise. "You're welcome!" he called with a friendly wave.

SCREECH!

SLAM!

CRASH!

That "friendly" wave caused the biggest frenzy yet—a fifteen-car pileup! Pedestrians nearly became speed bumps, horns were blaring, and tempers were flaring.

"Well, my work here is done," he said. Then he smiled. "What would this town do without me?"

SpongeBob was so pleased with his first hall monitor task, he had no idea that he had *caused* more accidents than he had prevented! He didn't notice all of the angry drivers, wrecked cars, and injured pedestrians around him.

"On patrol, I'm on patrol," he sang to himself as he left the traffic catastrophe.

chapter three

SpongeBob was walking home when he heard a noise. "Who's there?" SpongeBob said and froze. He looked at the looming shadow on the wall. "It's a bird . . . it's a plane . . . it's . . . it's . . . Hall Monitor!" he finished with a laugh.

SpongeBob walked a few more feet before another bold opportunity presented itself: a low, open window. "Uh-oh," he said and took a peek.

Inside the house, a couple of fish were enjoying a meal together.

"More seaweed medley, dear?" the female fish asked her husband.

"Oh, yes!" the husband replied. "You know it's my favorite!"

SpongeBob was appalled. "The fools! This open window is so unsafe! They've left themselves susceptible to danger."

Of course, SpongeBob couldn't just *warn* them of this danger. "I must show them the error of their ways . . . *by example!*" he declared.

SpongeBob looked around and grabbed a paper bag out of a nearby garbage can. He put it over his head, punching two holes out for eyes. Then he leaped in the window and screamed, "Oooooohhhh! I'm the Open-Window Maniac!"

"AHHHH!" screamed the husband and wife and ran for their lives.

"I hope you learned a valuable lesson!" SpongeBob called after them. He took a deep breath. "Boy, this hero stuff is hard work! But *someone* has to do it."

SpongeBob continued patrolling the streets of Bikini Bottom. He was so pleased with himself that he started to imagine his future. "With all I've done already, they should make me the permanent hall monitor. I can see it now . . . my picture in the Hall of Hall Monitors. Wanna-be hall monitors will hear stories of my brave monitoring experiences and I'll get the first-ever Hall Monitor medal. I'll give a speech at the Society of Hall Monitors. . . ."

Just then, something caught on SpongeBob's foot, causing him to fly through the air. "*WHOA!*" he yelled.

Once SpongeBob got to his feet, he shouted, "Vandals! Another crime!"

Before him on the ground was a blob of something pink. SpongeBob bent over and scooped up a dollop with his finger. "Mmmm . . . strawberry ice cream," he said, smelling it. "I must *act*! It's my duty as hall monitor to protect and serve. I must find out who's behind this delicious dessert . . . I mean, uh, crime!" He was looking around for any suspects when a dollop of the same strawberry ice cream fell on top of his head.

"Patrick!" exclaimed SpongeBob as he looked up and saw his best friend sitting on a wall.

Patrick looked around and didn't see anyone. He continued licking his ice cream.

"Patrick!" SpongeBob shouted again.

Patrick's eyes widened in fear. "My ice cream! It's alive!" he cried. "Aaaaaahhhhhh!!!" He threw the ice cream up in the air. It went high

in the sky, turned upside down, and started its descent—landing right in SpongeBob's face!

"Down here, Patrick," called SpongeBob, wiping his face.

Patrick looked down and smiled. "Oh, SpongeBob, it's you!"

"Come down here," SpongeBob ordered.

Getting off the wall wasn't too easy for Patrick. He lost his balance and landed right on top of SpongeBob, flattening him like a pancake.

"SpongeBob? SpongeBob, where are you?" Patrick called out.

In a muffled voice, SpongeBob said, "I'm down here!"

Patrick stood up and stared at SpongeBob. "You look funny, SpongeBob!" he said with a giggle.

"That's *Hall Monitor* to you," SpongeBob

corrected as he stood up and expanded back to his normal size.

"Oops. Sorry, Officer," replied Patrick.

"Sorry is not good enough, Patrick," SpongeBob told him. "You've just committed a crime and I'm taking you in!"

"What crime?" Patrick asked nervously.

"Littering!" SpongeBob declared. "Ice cream is meant to go in your mouth—not on the street."

Patrick burst into tears. "Oh, I'm a bad person!" he sobbed. "Boo hoo! Boo hoo!"

Just then a fish selling newspapers approached the pair. "Extra! Extra! Maniac strikes Bikini Bottom! City paralyzed with fear!" he cried and handed them a newspaper. "Take it, friends. Arm yourselves with knowledge!"

SpongeBob began to read. "Hmmm . . .

maniac . . . Bikini Bottom . . . car wrecks . . . a break-in . . ." Then he took a breath and said in his most heroic voice, "Who better to bring this maniac to justice than me . . . Hall Monitor!"

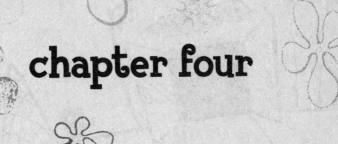

chapter four

SpongeBob turned to Patrick, who was still upset about the ice cream incident. "I can't handle this maniac case alone,". SpongeBob explained. "Patrick! Are you ready to give up your life of crime?"

"I want to be GOOD!" cried Patrick.

"Uh-huh. I thought so!" SpongeBob said, proud of his best buddy. "Now you just need a symbol of authority," he added, looking around.

Patrick picked up the ice-cream cone from the ground and put in on his head. It fit perfectly!

"Excellent!" said SpongeBob. "It is our duty to catch this maniac and bring him to justice. But how to proceed?" He looked over at Patrick. "Hey, Deputy, you're an excriminal, what would you do?"

"Hmmm," Patrick thought carefully. "I know! I'd get an ice cream!"

"Let's go!" said SpongeBob.

A little while later, SpongeBob and Patrick emerged from the ice-cream parlor. They each had an ice-cream cone and seventy-five little taster spoons.

Soon they both had licked their ice creams until they were all gone.

"Okay, now what?" asked SpongeBob.

"Seconds?" suggested Patrick.

"I'm ready!" said SpongeBob and they headed back inside.

"Thirds?" Patrick suggested a few minutes later.

"Sure!" replied SpongeBob.

Seven ice creams later, SpongeBob finally said, "Patrick, this isn't working. We're not getting any closer to catching the maniac."

"Yeah," agreed Patrick. "But this ice cream sure is tasty!"

"We've got to do something else," SpongeBob declared. "Something with . . . walkie-talkies!"

"Yaaayy!" cheered Patrick.

SpongeBob pulled out two walkie-talkies, handing one to Patrick. "I think we'll have a better chance of catching the maniac if we split up."

"Awww," Patrick said, disappointed.

SpongeBob put a hand on Patrick's shoulder. In his best hall monitor voice he said, "Remember, it's for the good of the mission, son. After all, there's a maniac on the loose!"

Patrick sighed. "Yeah, I guess so."

"Now duty calls," said SpongeBob. "I'll go that way. Deputy, you go . . . some other way! Roll 'em out!" SpongeBob did his best imitation of a siren as he left. "Wee-oo! Wee-oo! Wee-oo! Wee-oo! Wee-oo! Wee-oo!"

The next thing Patrick knew, a *real* police vehicle pulled up to him.

"Afternoon, son," one cop said to Patrick.

Patrick smiled. "Hello, brothers!" he replied, signaling to his cone hat.

The police officers exchanged puzzled looks with each other. They both wondered what they could possibly have in common with this overstuffed starfish.

Pressing on, one cop said, "We're looking for the maniac."

The other officer stuck a wanted poster in front of Patrick's face and asked, "Have you seen this guy?"

"Aaaaaaaaah!" Patrick screamed. He couldn't believe how horrible and frightening the maniac looked. His eyes were as black as coal. His rectangular, yellow body radiated menace. Patrick couldn't stand it anymore. "Take him away! Take him away!" he shouted.

"Calm down, son!" said one of the officers. "It's just a *drawing*. It's not the real thing."

Patrick breathed a small sigh of relief.

The police officer continued, "Now we're going to show you this drawing of the maniac again and you tell us if you've seen him. Understand?"

"Yeah! Uh-huh!" Patrick replied.

"Okay," said the cop. "Here we go."

"Aaaah! Horrible!" Patrick screamed again. "Take him away!"

The cop quickly took away the drawing. Both officers looked at Patrick and then at each other. Then one of the officers held the drawing up to Patrick again.

"Aaaah!" Patrick shouted.

The officer took away the drawing and Patrick seemed to instantly calm down.

Then the officer showed it to him again.

"Aaaah!" Patrick shouted.

The officer took it away. Patrick was calm. The police officers gave each other a sly look and grinned.

Finally the cops had had enough entertainment for one day and put the wanted poster away.

"Stay *indoors,* son," one cop warned Patrick.

Then the other cop added, "And, uh, take that stupid cone off your head!" Both officers snickered as they drove away.

chapter five

Patrick was spooked. He immediately pulled out his walkie-talkie. "SpongeBob!" he called into it. "SpongeBob, come in! Answer!"

"SpongeBob here. Patrick, report," said SpongeBob.

"I don't want to be a police officer anymore! I'm *scared!*" Patrick cried. "There's a maniac on the prowl!"

SpongeBob tried to calm Patrick down. "Get ahold of yourself, Deputy!"

"Bwaaa! Boo hoo!" sobbed Patrick. "I want to go home!"

Poor rookie, SpongeBob thought sadly to himself. Then through his walkie-talkie he told Patrick, "All right, all right. I'm on my way back."

"Hurry, SpongeBob!" Patrick said. "I think it's getting . . . dark!"

And just like that, it was dark.

"Put on your siren," SpongeBob told Patrick. "I'll be right there."

Patrick shivered with fear as he walked down the street. In a scared voice, he whispered, "Wee . . . woo . . . wee . . . woo . . . wee . . . woo . . ."

Patrick bent down and picked up something. It was a wanted poster for the maniac. When Patrick looked up from the poster, he saw something else—something even scarier. "WEE WOO! WEE WOO! WEE WOO!" he shouted.

In the distance, Patrick *saw* the maniac! Standing under a streetlight, the Maniac looked as scary and dangerous as his picture on the wanted poster.

"SpongeBob!" Patrick cried into his walkie-talkie. "I *see* him!"

"The maniac?" SpongeBob radioed back.

"Uh-huh!" Patrick responded.

"Where is he, Patrick?" SpongeBob asked.

Patrick looked up at the street signs. "At the intersection of Conch and Coral," he said.

"That's where I am!" declared SpongeBob, getting frightened. "He's right on top of me, but I just can't see him. It's too dark. What's he doing, Patrick?"

Patrick peered into the distance. "Uh . . . he's just standing there . . . *menacingly!*" he

reported. "Get out of there, SpongeBob!"

"Aaaaahhhh!" SpongeBob cried and began running around looking for a place to hide.

In the distance, Patrick heard a horrible cry. He grew even more afraid. "That's his maniac shriek! He's going to attack!" he shouted into his walkie-talkie.

"Patrick, help!" SpongeBob shouted as he ran in circles, growing more and more afraid.

"The maniac's actin' all crazy! RUN!" Patrick instructed.

SpongeBob quickly darted behind a building.

"No! Wait! The maniac's behind that building!" Patrick yelled.

"Yikes!" yelled SpongeBob and hightailed it behind a street sign.

"The maniac just went behind the sign!" Patrick yelled.

SpongeBob ran to a streetlight. He literally picked it up to hide underneath it.

"Wait! Now he's under the streetlight!" Patrick shrieked.

"AAAAAAHHHH!" screamed SpongeBob.

"RUN FOR YOUR LIFE!" Patrick yelled.

SpongeBob was sobbing when he spotted the perfect hiding place. "Aha!" he said and dove headfirst into a mailbox. Among the layers of letters, SpongeBob breathed a sigh of relief.

Suddenly SpongeBob heard Patrick's voice on the walkie-talkie. The walkie-talkie was buried beneath the letters, so the reception wasn't clear.

"Say again, Deputy?" SpongeBob radioed.

"The maniac's in the mailbox!" Patrick repeated.

"YEEOOOWWW!" SpongeBob screamed.

He punched holes in the sides and bottom of the mailbox for his arms and legs. Now wearing the mailbox, SpongeBob began to run, but he couldn't see where he was going. He ran through buildings and homes, trying to get away from the dreaded maniac.

WHAM!

SpongeBob crashed right into a fence. The mailbox split open on impact, and SpongeBob found himself surrounded by the planks of the fence he had just broken through.

"I can't see! I can't see!" he shrieked.

But then SpongeBob opened his eyes and found that there was a piece of paper covering his face. It was one of the wanted posters for the maniac.

"Huh! This guy's not half bad looking for a maniac," SpongeBob thought aloud as he looked at it.

Suddenly SpongeBob saw the resemblance. "Wait a minute, Patrick . . . *I'm* the maniac!"

A line of police officers immediately appeared.

"We'll take *that* as a confession!" declared one officer.

"But . . . I . . . uh . . . ," began SpongeBob.

Just then, Mrs. Puff showed up on the scene. She made her way to SpongeBob. "SpongeBob SquarePants! *There* you are! I turn my back on you for one minute and you destroy half the city. You should be ashamed of yourself!"

"You know this guy?" a cop asked Mrs. Puff.

"Of course I do!" replied Mrs. Puff. "I'm the one who gave him the uniform in the first place. He's *my* responsibility!"

All the police officers narrowed their eyes at Mrs. Puff.

"Uh-oh!" Mrs. Puff said, realizing she had just taken the blame for SpongeBob and all the trouble he had caused. "This is going on your permanent record, SpongeBob!" she called as the police carted her away.

In class the next day, an embarrassed SpongeBob kept to himself. Everyone in Bikini Bottom had heard about his hall monitor fiasco—or had unintentionally been a part of it. As Mrs. Puff finished her lesson for the day, SpongeBob made sure to take precise notes.

"And in conclusion, students," Mrs. Puff said, "red means stop. Green means go. And SpongeBob . . ."

SpongeBob looked up at the TV monitor sitting on top of Mrs. Puff's desk. "Yes, Mrs. Puff?"

"I'd like to see you after class . . . *six months from now!*" snapped Mrs. Puff from her jail cell.

SpongeBob meekly replied, "Yes, Mrs. Puff." He knew now that he had no chance of being hall monitor—*ever again!*

The End

AHOY THERE, KIDS! HERE'S A SNEAK PEEK AT
CHAPTER BOOK #4: *THE WORLD'S GREATEST VALENTINE*
IN THE SPONGEBOB SQUAREPANTS SERIES.
IT'S A SPLASHY TALE. . . .

"Happy Valentine's Day, Bikini Bottom!" With this jaunty cry SpongeBob SquarePants sprang out the front door of his pineapple home and ran across the ocean floor.

SpongeBob had thought February 14 would never arrive! His skinny arms were filled to overflowing with valentines of all shapes and sizes. After weeks of waiting, he could deliver his custom-made gifts at last!

"First stop, a valentine for my favorite next-door neighbor!" SpongeBob said with a happy giggle.

Dancing across the sea grass on the tiptoes of his shiny patent leather shoes, SpongeBob lobbed a large pink valentine into the lap of his frowning neighbor, Squidward.

"Happy Valentine's Day, pal!" SpongeBob sang. "Will you be mine?"

Squidward scowled, then sat back in his outdoor lounge chair. "Why don't you go play in shark-infested waters?" he suggested sarcastically.

"That's a great idea! Sharks need

love too, and I've got lots more valentines to give!" SpongeBob replied with a wave. "Good-bye!"

"Good riddance," Squidward said sourly, shredding his valentine into confetti and tossing the pieces over his head.

Spotting Mrs. Puff behind the steering wheel of her blue-and-white motorboat, SpongeBob ran up alongside her vehicle.

"Happy Valentine's Day, Mrs. Puff!" SpongeBob called as he tossed her a red valentine with white lace.

"Oh, my! Thank you, SpongeBob!" the flustered blowfish replied as she opened the valentine.

"I get a bang out of you," Mrs. Puff read, not paying attention to where she was going. . . .

Crunch! Mrs. Puff drove right into a fire hydrant!

Pwooosh! Her body inflated to four times its normal size!

Luckily, Mrs. Puff wasn't injured in the accident thanks to her "built-in" air bag!

SpongeBob didn't hear the wreck. He was already dropping off another valentine.

Taking out a pair of tweezers, he selected the smallest paper heart from his pile and held it out to a tiny green creature with one bulging red eye.

"SpongeBob!" the evil Plankton cried as he looked up. "So, Mr. Krabs has sent you to destroy me! Well, I'm ready for you! Give me your best shot!"

"Okay!" SpongeBob agreed. "Here you go!"

Plankton took the offering and read the note aloud. "I'd walk the plank for you! Be my valentine! Love . . . SpongeBob?"

"Ha ha ha ha!" SpongeBob tittered as he skipped away. "Happy Valentine's Day, Plankton!"

"Curse you, SpongeBob!" Plankton boomed, hopping up and down with anger. "Curse you!"

SpongeBob wasn't listening. He

continued dropping off valentines throughout Bikini Bottom. But he had to hurry, for there was a final stop to make before his Valentine's Day was complete. . . .

about the author

For **Annie Auerbach**, it's been a wild ride from a background in theater and film to a career in publishing. Besides being an editor for a Los Angeles publishing company, she is also a freelance writer and the author of books based on Nickelodeon's *CatDog*, Disney's *A Bug's Life*, and many more. She's now grateful that her parents limited her TV viewing time as a kid—telling her to read a book instead!